DANGEROUSLY
CLOSE TO HOME

Other Close to Home Books
by John McPherson

Close to Home

DANGEROUSLY
CLOSE TO HOME
BY JOHN McPHERSON

ZondervanPublishingHouse
Grand Rapids, Michigan

A Division of HarperCollinsPublishers

To Peter

"I want to apologize to you guys for the little mix-up we've had with the uniforms. I'll be talking to the ballet instructor, and with any luck we'll get things cleared up before the big game on Saturday."

Mike would know better than to raise his hand
the next time Mr. Ferncod asked for a
volunteer to erase the blackboard.

"But until we find exactly where the
hamster crawled off to and died, thank heavens
for these little stick-on air fresheners."

8

9

"We must have looked at 50 recliners, but Al wanted this one because of its automatic comfort settings."

Though Louise tried to be discreet, people quickly homed in on the source of the microwave popcorn aroma.

"Well, how did it go at the vet's? Did the cat put up much of a fuss?"

"I told my parents I had to have a phone in my room, so they moved all of my stuff into the living room."

"So far, five diaper services have canceled us."

Being the person who selects a video for the night is a position of awesome responsibility.

"Oh, nonsense! It doesn't look silly at all!
When you've got a head cold as bad as yours,
it's important to be prepared!"

"Oh, I forgot to tell you. Your father just installed
a security system to warn him anytime somebody
sets the temperature above 65 degrees."

"So I said, 'I don't care if it's an $800 option, I want the shatter-resistant, soundproof barrier.'"

16

"The computer system is down again."

"I *told* you! I can't do the laundry *or* use the stove!
The allergy medicine I'm on says not to
operate heavy equipment."

"For the last time, Watkins, you *cannot*
have the day after Thanksgiving off!"

18

"I told Ed this was a ridiculous mobile to get a 7-month-old, but he says it's a necessity if she's going to have any chance of getting into Harvard Medical School in 2014."

Not long into the date, Dave began to sense some negative vibes from Glenda.

"We're training him to go only on the newspaper."

20

Although half the team was out with the flu, the Fighting Pigeons of Varnberg High did their best to make their opponents think they were at full strength.

"Isn't there a snooze button somewhere on him that we can hit?"

"We kept losing the other remote."

"I need a card that says, 'Sorry I used your new bathrobe to wax the car.'"

"There. *Now* it's halftime. What do you say we all go to the table and have a nice, quiet Thanksgiving dinner."

23

After months of study, management reveals the new reorganization plan.

"Don't just shove that back in there any old place! I just alphabetized everything in the refrigerator."

"We know that $2,800 is a lot to spend on a clock, but we couldn't resist once they showed us this engraved signature: 'Ben Franklin, 1752'!"

"I got some of that hair that comes in a spray can, but I wanted to test it on the dog first."

"I thought the family rental rate was too good to be true."

Despite his bad back, Wayne held to tradition by making sure
his bride was carried over the threshold.

27

"Oh, you mean this? My dad's on this big kick lately about making sure we turn out lights when we leave a room."

"He's not much of a watchdog, but he's great with kids."

28

It's never hard to spot the spouses at the annual office Christmas party.

"For cryin' out loud, will you just give it up and pay the three bucks?"

Hockey in heaven

"Looks like Mom and Dad are serious about us not shaking the presents this year."

Mrs. Mortleman made sure that everyone participated in class.

"Locked your keys in the house again, eh?"

Nobody could clip coupons like Helen Struman.

"For heaven's sake! Would it kill you
to go out and cut a little firewood?!"

"No chance of the cat knocking
the tree over *this* year."

"For Pete's sake, watch where you're going!
A foot more to the left and you would have
put a ski right through my new curtains!"

In a matter of seconds, Steve's social life
was reduced to that of pond scum.

"It just got to the point where it was impossible to keep track of all the kids, so Dan had the control center installed."

"You'll probably find this considerably more strenuous than other treadmill tests you've taken."

Purchasing a new phone these days can spark some heated negotiations.

"My blow dryer is broken."

Suddenly, Diane realized the incredible
power that she had.

39

Although they admired Chuck's dedication, the others in his car pool reminded him that it was 6:49 and perhaps he should start thinking about driving them all home.

"I lost my whistle."

"Unbelievable! I pump 14 tubes of caulk into a 3-inch gap in the siding and it's still not filled up!"

"**Here's how it works: If the ball hits the floor in your cubicle, you've gotta be on call for the weekend.**"

"Will you quit buying these darned 'LOVE' stamps?!
I feel like a hypocrite whenever I pay the electric bill!"

"Take it easy! It's a clean sock! What'd you expect
me to do when we're out of coffee filters?"

"Sometimes I worry that your mom doesn't get enough exercise."

Bud saved a bundle by making Christmas gifts for his family in metal shop.

"It says on your résumé that you can type 260 words per minute. No offense, Mrs. Ballas, but I find that pretty hard to believe."

"I told Ed we needed more closet space, so he installed a door made out of Spandex."

Despite an 0-and-14 season and slumping attendance, loyal Pigeons fans still showed their support by doing the Wave.

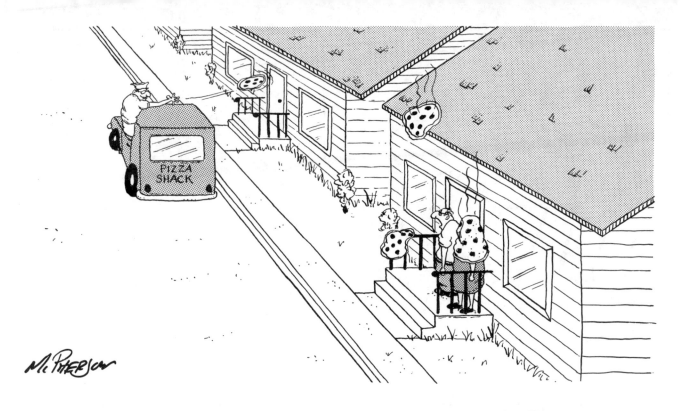

"Didn't that pizza delivery kid used to be our paperboy?"

"And over here's our family snow shovel.
This baby can clear a driveway in no time."

"The kid in 4C got a BB gun for Christmas."

"Oh, yeah? Well, *my* digital watch tells the temperature, humidity, my cholesterol level and blood pressure, and the current Dow-Jones industrial average."

"No, that's not what I said. I said I made a New Year's resolution not to eat dinner in my underwear *when your mother is here*."

"It's part of the company's new emphasis on health and fitness."

"OK, let's have one more shot. This time, try not to look directly at the flash."

"All right! Who's the dingbat who used the phone last?!"

Unable to find a Hi-Liter, Wayne Merlman used a black Magic Marker to cross out all the stuff he didn't want to read again.

"My burger's still a little pink on the inside.
Hold the cigarette lighter up to it for a
couple of minutes, would ya?"

54

At the Minivan Owners Support Group

"You want your coffee warmed up a bit?"

"The rest of the bell choir is out with the flu."

"I saved the new jumbo slide carousel for last!"

"There's no such thing as the Toenail Fairy, bonehead!"

Birthday phobia. Stage One: Denial

Vern messes up his right-turn signal again.

"Do we still have the warranty for my razor?"

The inevitable result of going for weeks without untangling your phone cord.

"And so, in appreciation of his suggestion, which will save the company more than $350,000 annually, I am honored to present Al Wimbot with this exquisite stainless-steel tire gauge, engraved with the company's logo!"

"Yes, it is kind of like having a giant puppet. Now let Daddy get some sleep.
You can play with him again after lunch."

"Nah, we never clean it out. Once a year we just stick a sign in the yard that says 'Garage Sale.'"

"With five kids in the house, this was the only way we could think of to give everybody a fair shot at the bathroom."

"You better get those bindings checked out when you get back to the lodge. Those things should have released after a wipeout like this."

"That's my Uncle Vinnie. The organist
called in sick at the last minute."

For people who never remember it's garbage day until the truck passes their house, Zamco's new Garbage-Sling 2000 is a must.

"I couldn't afford to get airbags as an option. If it looks like we're going to hit something, start blowing these up."

"We haven't changed those sheets in ages."

"Tommy? He's upstairs in his room having 'time out.'"

"I'll be going to the Bahamas for a week starting tomorrow. This should tide you over 'til I get back."

"I couldn't find a ladder."

"Maybe you haven't heard, Karl, but it's sort of a tradition around here that whoever wins the 50 bucks in the Super Bowl pool takes the rest of the office out to lunch."

"Who did you say did your bypass surgery?"

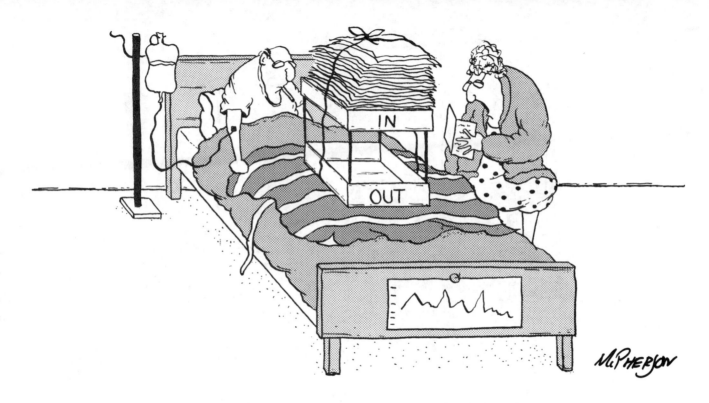

"It's from your boss. It says, 'Best wishes for a speedy recovery.'"

"I finally decided that the only way to keep the kids' socks straight in the laundry was to number them."

"All right! I think I finally got this
stupid drain unplugged!"

"Noreen's having a tough time coping
with the empty nest syndrome."

73

"Some guy from the Department of Public Works came over and installed it this morning. The city's trying to raise enough money for a new skating rink."

"Could we have separate checks? On one put me, the woman down there in the weird glasses, and that kid at the other end putting the straw in his ear. On another, the guy with the bad hairpiece, the woman..."

74

Bob would go to any lengths to get that promotion.

"Let us know if you want a little more legroom back there."

"I've been cooking in bulk to save money. Just tell me
how much spaghetti you want me to reel off."

76

By marking the volleyball with red paint, referees at Pilburn College were able to avoid heated disputes over line calls.

"There! Now you've got no reason to wake us up
at 3 A.M. asking for a glass of water."

"Yep, I got this beauty used from that amusement
park over in Elmira. Made out like a bandit!"

"Hey, what do you care? They give you free refills."

Although convenient, having your desk near the coffeemaker has some definite drawbacks.

"I can never remember to water those darned plants."

"What d'ya mean this highway is closed?! If it's closed, then why on earth don't they have the decency to warn a person?!"

"Their 4-year-old just got potty-trained."

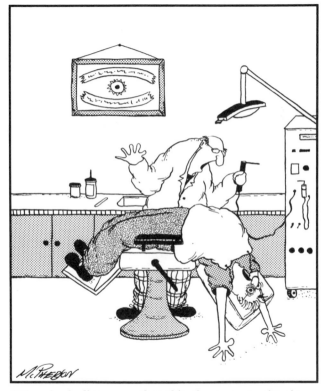

"Hey, look, I'm sorry that this gives you a migraine, but it makes it a heck of a lot easier for me to get to those upper molars."

"I don't care if it's a nice-looking vest! It was a
sport coat when I brought it in here!"

84

"Here's something that should knock out that head cold. I got you some of that new deep sinus decongestant."

"Jim, we've worked together for 17 years. You know I've always respected your opinions, but the entire department, including me, feels you're way off base here. That's definitely Waldo hiding in the coal mine, not in the dump truck, as you keep insisting."

"OK, cover me!"

"I tell you! These hide-a-key rocks are just the cleverest things!"

"I thought of getting a backpack, but they cost a fortune, so I just made outfits for me and Leon out of Velcro and voilà!"

Mr. Gickman wasn't too good with names.

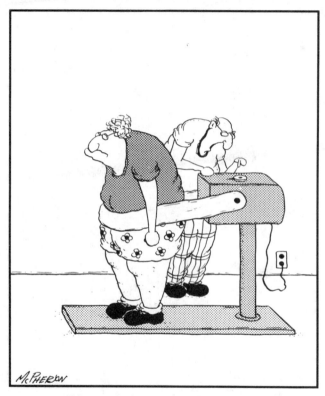

"You want it set on low, medium,
or high or industrial strength?"

Yet another example of the credit card companies'
aggressive attempts to attract new cardholders.

"This is what I get for requesting an
office with a window."

"Don't expect sympathy from me! I've been telling
you for months that we need a humidifier!"

"When you take into account rest stops for me, Louise, and the kids,
I figure that towing the porta-john will save us about 50 minutes a day."

"Boys will be boys!"

"OK! Put the dead spider in that cube,
the centipede there, and the chipmunk foot in
that one. Then we stick the tray in the freezer and
watch the expressions on everybody's faces at
Mom and Dad's big party Saturday night!"

93

"Did you ever notice that when you dial your
parents' phone number, it sounds like the
theme to 'The Addams Family'?"

"Must be the pizza delivery kid that we
forgot to tip last week."

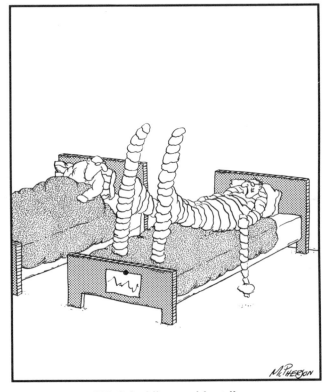

"Me? A skiing accident."

94

"Sorry, Dad. We got a little carried away with the snowman building."

"Yep, here it is right in the lease: 'Refrigerator shall be shared equally between tenants in apartments 4A and 4B'."

Wayne's latest metal-shop project dramatically changed the course of pillow fights in the Milner household forever.

"Oh, for heaven's sake! It's Stan and Lois Murdock from New Year's weekend!"

The SAT: the ultimate test of a student's intelligence.

The new converging conference room walls helped to keep meetings from dragging on indefinitely.

"Oh, for heaven's sake! This thing has been on *reverse* the whole time!"

"Sorry, sir, but something is still setting off the metal detector."

"That's not a twist-off cap."

Based on the computer calculations he had run, Lowell needed to hit the ceiling at an angle of 37 degrees in order to land his rubber band in Milt's coffee.

"Once again, we're very sorry about the mix-up. We can have your furniture here in eight days. However, we've spoken to the Mulners in Anchorage, and they say they actually prefer your furniture and are wondering if you're interested in an even swap."

Despite their popularity, many of the fancy new mall hair salons just don't have the personal touch of the old neighborhood barber shops.

"Look, I know you hate it, but until I get a chance to put some nonslip decals in the tub, I'd feel a lot better if you'd just wear the helmet."

"My 17-year-old drove the car into the garage door three times, so I finally just said the heck with it and installed the beads."

"Don't worry, it's not a real tattoo. I just want to see the look on Dad's face when he brings his boss home for tonight's big dinner."

"For God's sake, call a plumber!"

"Sweep it up? What the heck for?
It makes great insulation!"

"We just locked our baby-sitter into an exclusive
three-year contract prohibiting her from sitting for
anyone else. After that she's eligible for free agency."

"It's times like these that make me hate technology."

"My mother always said, 'You can never have too much counter space.'"

As the only employees in the office who didn't have daughters selling **Girl Scout** cookies, Ron and Greg were hunted down like animals.

"I've been going over our finances. According to my calculations, our monthly retirement income will be either $2,124 or $42,798, depending on whether or not we win the **Publishers Clearing House** sweepstakes."

"It cost $45, but you shouldn't need to buy deodorant again until you're 68!"

"Boy, that was something! I don't know who was more surprised, you or that deer!"

"Right now the baby is *not* in the proper position for delivery, but I'm confident it will shift in time for your due date."

"We discovered that if we reverse the wires and yell into the TV, we can talk to the space shuttle crew."

After the team lost 20 consecutive games, Coach Farnsworth did his best to help his players regain their confidence.

"I'm trying to figure out which of these wires carries the
Home Shopping Network so I can cut it."

Charlene soon began to realize that being the teacher's pet wasn't all it was cracked up to be.

Howard offers his opinion regarding the office's new piped-in elevator music.

**"Oh, wait! Here's the problem!
The hose was kinked!"**

"No, really. Be honest."

"Man! That was one *mean* pothole!"

"For cryin' out loud, if you like the smell of the cologne in the ad, go out and buy some of it!"

"We wanted to get him one of those marble-tower kits, but we were worried that he might swallow a marble."

"Once again, I want to stress that the story I just related during my sermon is *purely* fictional and is no way based upon anyone here in the congregation."

"I arranged my flex time so that I'll work 14 hours a day, six days a week, and then get 1998 off."

"The CD player is messed up again."

After trying for 25 minutes to get their check,
Ed was finally able to get their waiter's attention.

"I told Stan that the ceiling was leaking again,
and this was his solution."

119

Algebra teacher Bert Fegman was a master of reverse psychology.

"Oh, isn't that *darling!* She's telling you how old she is!"

Friends had warned Bert not to join a CD club.

New employees were quick to notice the little cliques that existed at the P. L. Fernley Co.

Budget conference call

"Stick the other end of this in your mouth and say 'Ahh.'"

One of the hazards of renting a car.

After hitting seven consecutive shots into the pond,
Rick began to show a hint of apathy
toward his golf game.

Corporate manager Hank Clemmer firmly believes that a comfortable employee is a lazy employee.

Recent advancements in ultrasound technology have resulted in extremely accurate reports.

Unfortunately, Bernice didn't read the washing instructions on her new blouse until she got it home.

"I admit, I was apprehensive when Alan first talked about getting an industrial-strength garbage disposal, but now I don't know how we got by without it."

As the band continued to play, an angry mob searched for members of the prom committee.

"Talk about perfect timing! I just happened to walk out here with the camcorder just as that rung broke!"

"That settles it! No catnip for *that* cat!"

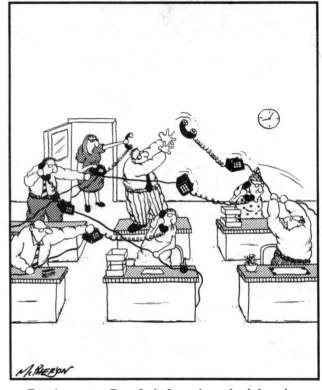

**Employees at Bumfarb Associates hadn't quite
mastered the fine art of transferring phone calls.**